Chihuahuas

Sarah Frank

Lerner Publications • Minneapolis

Lerner Publications Company
A division of Lerner Publishing Group, Inc.
241 First Avenue North
Minneapolis, MN 55401 USA

For reading levels and more information, look up this title at www.lernerbooks.com.

Library of Congress Cataloging-in-Publication Data

Names: Frank, Sarah, author.
Title: Chihuahuas / Sarah Frank.
Description: Minneapolis : Lerner Publications, [2019] | Series: Lightning bolt books. who's a good dog? | Audience: Ages 6–9. | Audience: K to Grade 3. | Includes bibliographical references and index.
Identifiers: LCCN 2018035859 (print) | LCCN 2018037591 (ebook) | ISBN 9781541556638 (eb pdf) | ISBN 9781541555730 (lb : alk. paper)
Subjects: LCSH: Chihuahua (Dog breed)—Juvenile literature. | Dogs—Juvenile literature.
Classification: LCC SF429.C45 (ebook) | LCC SF429.C45 F73 2019 (print) | DDC 636.76—dc23

LC record available at https://lccn.loc.gov/2018035859

Manufactured in the United States of America
1-46028-43351-11/27/2018

Table of Contents

Small and Super!

Good things come in tiny packages. A Chihuahua is proof of that!

Most kids have teddy bears bigger than a Chihuahua.

Chihuahuas are the world's smallest dogs. They are about 5 inches (13 cm) tall. They weigh about 5 pounds (2.3 kg).

Do you like long-haired or short-haired Chihuahuas best?

Some Chihuahuas have short, smooth coats. Others have long coats. Chihuahuas also can be different colors.

Chihuahuas aren't only cute. They are feisty and fearless too. But most of all, they love their owners.

Tiny Toys

The American Kennel Club (AKC) groups dogs by breed. Dogs that have things in common are grouped together. Tiny Chihuahuas are in the toy group.

Toy dogs don't all look alike. But all of them are small enough to sit on your lap.

Toy dogs come from countries around the world. Chihuahuas came to the United States from Mexico. Americans visiting Mexico in the nineteenth century brought the dogs home as pets.

Chihuahuas are still favorite pets in the United States.

Some Chihuahuas are more than pets. They also work as hearing dogs. These dogs help people who have trouble hearing. Other Chihuahuas compete in dog shows.

Your New Pet?

Chihuahua puppies are adorable. But that doesn't mean everyone should get one. Decide with an adult in your family if the breed is right for you.

Do you dream of jogging with your dog? If so, don't get a Chihuahua. These little dogs get enough exercise from simple games of fetch.

Your Chihuahua may need a sweater on cooler days.

Do you live in a cold place? Chihuahuas get cold easily. Going out in the snow or rain is not for them.

Do you have lots of spare time? You'll need it if you want a Chihuahua. These dogs aren't happy unless they spend tons of time with you.

Chihuahuas don't like to be alone.

Best Day Ever

Let's say your family still wants a Chihuahua. That's great! Get ready for the special day your dog comes home. Buy supplies such as a collar and dog bowls.

Vets take good care of pets.

Next, make a vet appointment for your furry friend. The vet will give your dog a checkup. It's important for your pet's health.

Healthful food is important for your dog.

Ask your vet what food your dog should eat. Many Chihuahuas are picky eaters. Your vet may know what your dog will like.

Welcome your Chihuahua to the family. Spend extra time with it in its first week at home. Soon you'll be the very best of friends!

Doggone Good Tips!

- Looking for the perfect name for your perfect pet? Here are some ideas: Elf, Pixie, Peanut, Burly, Bits, or Brawny.

- Chihuahuas don't warm up to strangers quickly. That goes for people as well as other animals. If you're inviting new people or pets into your home, give your Chihuahua space until it gets used to the extra company.

- Some people are surprised to learn that Chihuahuas make great watchdogs. They have super hearing and will bark if a stranger comes too near your home.

Why Chihuahuas Are the Best

- They look great in clothing! Many Chihuahua owners like to put bows in their dog's hair or dress it in cute sweaters. There are even Chihuahua fashion shows in some cities.

- Some Chihuahuas are in show business. Have you seen the movie *Beverly Hills Chihuahua*? It stars one of these pint-size pooches.

- Chihuahuas can live for eighteen years or even longer. They can be your BFF for many years.

Glossary

American Kennel Club (AKC): an organization that groups dogs by breed

breed: a particular kind of dog

coat: a dog's hair

feisty: lively or very frisky

hearing dog: a dog that helps a person who is deaf or who has trouble hearing

toy group: a group of different types of dogs that are all small in size

vet: a doctor who treats animals

Further Reading

American Kennel Club
https://www.akc.org

American Society for the Prevention of Cruelty
to Animals
https://www.aspca.org

Bodden, Valerie. *Chihuahuas*. Mankato, MN: Creative
Education, 2018.

Boothroyd, Jennifer. *Hero Service Dogs*. Minneapolis:
Lerner Publications, 2017.

Schuh, Mari. *Chihuahuas*. Minneapolis: Bellwether
Media, 2016.

Index

Photo Acknowledgments

Image credits: Erik Lam/Shutterstock.com, p. 2; 5 second Studio/Shutterstock.com, p. 4; nata-lunata/Shutterstock.com, p. 5; Sergey Lavrentev/Shutterstock.com, p. 6; LightField Studios/Shutterstock.com, p. 7; taratynova.photo/Shutterstock.com, p. 9; IvanMikhaylov/ Getty Images, p. 10; Leon Neal/Getty Images, p. 11; dezy/Shutterstock.com, p. 12; otsphoto/ Shutterstock.com, p. 13; Anna Hoychuk/Shutterstock.com, p. 14; Piti Tan/Shutterstock.com, p. 15; Africa Studio/Shutterstock.com, p. 16; bymuratdeniz/Getty Images, p. 17; Vitaly Titov/ Shutterstock.com, p. 18; Tono Balaguer/Shutterstock.com, p. 19; cynoclub/Shutterstock.com, p. 22; GlobalP/Getty Images, p. 23.

Cover Images: Eric Isselee/Shutterstock.com.

Main body text set in Billy Infant regular 28/36. Typeface provided by SparkType.

24